For God's Sake, Mother!
The Long Goodbye

For God's Sake, Mother!
The Long Goodbye

JAN SPICER

StoryTerrace

Copyright © Jan Spicer

First print June 2022

www.StoryTerrace.com

CONTENTS

DEDICATION	7
WHY I WROTE THIS BOOK	11
DETERMINED OLD WOMAN	15
MUM	19
THE YEARLY DECENT MEAL	31
A LITTLE ABOUT ME	35
HOME AND AWAY	47
SHAME ON US	57
SID	63
I'M ALRIGHT; IT'S THE OTHERS	67
BUT I'M STILL ALIVE!	75
PRESENT DAY	79
THE POEM	95

DEDICATION

Dedicated to the memory of James William Rogers.

Dear Dad,
I love and miss you more every day.
Your death in 2007 marked the end of the *Jim and Kath* show, which would have been in its 69th season this year. In one memorable episode, on location in Cornwall, you surprised us by buying Mars bars – you'd be the first to admit you were a penny pincher!
As we walked away from the shop, Mum fell down some steps and badly cut her legs. Instead of helping, you stepped over her, took her Mars bar, and said, 'You won't want this then!'
'Bollocks,' Mum said to you while Pete and I (in hysterics) tried to help her up.
At home, you'd often say to Mum, 'Do us some egg, bacon, tomato and two of toast.'

FOR GOD'S SAKE, MOTHER!

Mum would begrudgingly oblige.
'This egg's broken,' you'd complain.
'Bollocks,' Mum would say.
I'm sure 'Egg, bacon, tomato and two of toast' will be your first request when you see Mum again. We all know what her first words to you will be!
I wish I could kiss you one last time to hear you tell me *I need a shave!*
You turned any situation into a comedy. This book shows why we need you more than ever.

Miss you Dad.

Mum and Dad, the good old days.

WHY I WROTE THIS BOOK

The 'Dementia Demon' entered our lives in 2018 in the form of a 'memory-eating' disease. We've watched it take our mum away, piece by piece.

This book shares our family's struggles with this cruel illness. In the UK alone, the number of people with dementia is estimated to be 850,000*. Therefore, dementia will try to destroy thousands more families; maybe you're reading this because your family member has been diagnosed.

If you'd be kind enough to accompany me on the downward-spiralling journey of self-loathing, unhappiness and guilt this demon has dragged us on, I hope to show you the love, learning, forgiveness and understanding we've gained on the way. We've made many mistakes since Mum's diagnosis, so perhaps this story will help you avoid making similar ones.

Our story is told with love and good intentions. It reveals the devastating home truths about vascular dementia and how we try to overcome the hurdles creeping up on us at an alarming rate.

This book is also about the fun and laughter we have and the importance of staying together as a family. You will laugh at the funny parts of our story that outshine our often hopeless desperation.

We are fortunate that we're able to rely on services and close family to help take care of Mum, yet obtaining support has been a journey in itself.

Surrender seems to be the proverbial 'light at the end of the tunnel'. Over the years, I have been able to accept and embrace Mum's 'diamentcha' (as she calls it) as part of her.

Sadly, it will continue to destroy Kathleen Elsie Rogers, until she is no more. This book is me collating the pieces we still have of Mum to protect them forever.

Parts of this book may cause offence. I use language that should not be used today. I would like the reader to bear in mind that in the 1930s and '40s (when Mum was brought up), 'political correctness' hadn't been invented.

(*Source NHS England.)

Last holiday picture, me (standing), Mum (centre), Wendy on her left and Jackie on her right.

DETERMINED OLD WOMAN

2017

Mum was asleep on the couch when I arrived. Her face was deathly white and cold to the touch. Fearing she'd died, I shook her on the shoulder. 'Mum, Mum, wake up! It's me, Jan!' Mum stirred. 'Oh! Hello, Jan,' she croaked.

Mum soon became more alert when I said, 'I will call an ambulance.'

Mum sat up and spoke. 'I'm not going to hospital!'

I had already called the emergency services; two paramedics were on their way.

'Let us check you over, Mrs Rogers,' said one paramedic, pulling up the skin on the back of her hand. 'She is dehydrated and a bit confused. Her blood pressure is high, and her pulse is racing,' he said. 'When was the last time she ate or drank?' My little sister Wendy, who had arrived at Mum's that morning, said she didn't know how long Mum had been like this.

'We need to get her to hospital,' said the paramedic.

'NOOOOOOOOO!' Mum shouted, her rudeness outshining her usual stubbornness (I mean, determination).

'I'm not going to hospital. Leave me alone. I can take care of myself.'

Wendy and I were so shocked; this outburst wasn't like Mum. Our other sister, Jackie, had arrived by now, and the three of us tried to persuade Mum she needed to go to the hospital.

'Don't worry, Mrs Rogers, you shouldn't be in there too long. You need hydrating to make you feel better,' said the paramedic as he tried again to reason with Mum. Mum was still having none of it. Like a spoilt child, she sat there with a stubborn (determined) look on her face.

'We have power of attorney over her health and wellbeing,' I stated. The paramedic gave me a look, a look that made me think I shouldn't have mentioned this. 'If your mum says no, she means no. We cannot force her to go in the ambulance, power of attorney or not!' He put me in my place.

'Is there something your mum would eat?' asked the other paramedic. Instantly, Mum sat up and retorted, 'I'll have a bowl of porridge and a cup of tea.'

All three sisters and the paramedics were stunned into silence. *Bloody hell, Mum. Why do you do this to us?* I thought to myself.

We left Mum with the paramedics and went into the kitchen. It had taken three-quarters of an hour for Mum to agree to eat.

Before the paramedics left, one of them asked, 'Does your mum have dementia?'

Mum with Wendy and Jackie.

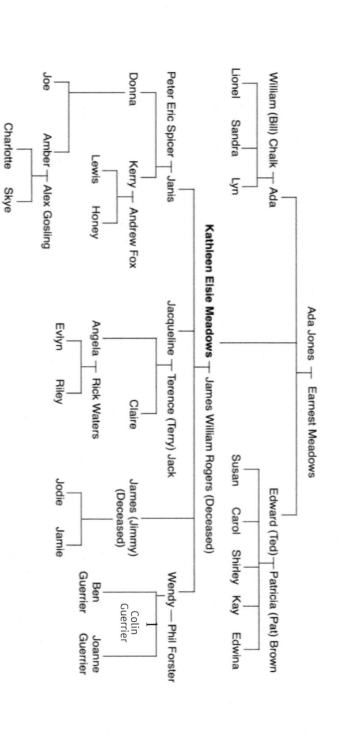

MUM

On 3rd December 1934, Kathleen Elsie was born to Ada and Ernest Meadows, a baby sister for Ada, seven, and Ted, five. Grandad Earnest died of consumption when Mum was only 14. Nanny Ada was left raising a strong-willed teenager. As a young child during the war, Mum was evacuated to Cornwall. Mum recalled the happy times living in Nanstallon, a small village outside Bodmin. The couple looking after her wanted to adopt her and start a new life in Canada.

If Nanny Ada hadn't fetched her back, I'd have had a Canadian accent!

Mum had a lovely childhood being spoilt by her siblings. A black and white photo hangs on the wall of our family home of Nanny Ada and Mum's sister standing in the background while Mum is in the forefront holding a lead attached to a large black dog. Now, before continuing, I need to explain I do not agree with using offensive or racist words, but in the 1940s, words were not deemed racist or discriminatory. Nowadays, hearing someone calling, 'Nigger, Nigger, come here boy,' would result in arrests. I forgive Mum's family for naming their dog Nigger, and hope you will do too.

Happily Ever After

Mum used to take her sister's clothes and high-heel shoes and meet her friends at Chislehurst Caves, trying to attract the attention of young soldiers who were on leave. Mum used to rush home afterwards and get her brother to clean the shoes she had 'borrowed' before Ada got home from work, so that Ada would not know!

Mum met James William Rogers, Dad, at Chislehurst Caves, when he was on army leave. They married on 28th November 1953, when she was 17 years old. I was there too, a tiny being in her tummy.

I was born in June 1954, seven months after Mum and Dad got married. Jackie was born the following year, in July 1955. Obviously, no televisions back in those days! When Dad left the army, there were no council houses available, so Mum, Dad, my baby sister and I lived at Nanny Ada's. Nan slept downstairs with our family of four, while Uncle Ted, Aunt Pat and their girls had the remaining two rooms upstairs!

The only way Nan could get her place back was to serve an eviction notice on us all! A lot of London had been bombed, so we moved into a prefab, where Mum, Dad, Jackie and I lived as a family of four for three years.

In the early '60s, Bedens Field Council Estate was built; Mum and Dad moved into 3 Fowlers Close. During this time, two more siblings arrived, Jimmy and Wendy. The house was full. The close had 12 houses. Mum is still there after 63 years, the only original resident in that close.

Back then, we didn't have to lock our doors and we kids played knock down ginger, hopscotch, football and skipping until dark.

We were always afraid of the 'fat' old lady, Mrs Plummer. My brother would yell, 'You can't catch us, fat cow!' after retrieving a ball that had gone over the fence. We all ran into our houses and watched from our bedroom window as an obese Mrs Plummer wobbled down the street, her round face red with anger.

'Wait till your father gets home,' must have been the most used phrase during our childhood.

Mum would spend most of the day in her bed, dreaming of Elvis, her one true love, the man she would have left us all for. She didn't seem to care what we got up to, as long she didn't have to entertain us herself.

The Jim and Kath Show

At 15, before Mum met Dad, she worked in a Dairylea cheese factory. They'd take their own bread in, toast it and hold it under the nozzle where the cheese came out! When Jimmy and Wendy started school, Mum worked evenings at Kolster-Brandes in Foots Cray, a thriving factory manufacturing radio and television sets. Mum loved getting away from the responsibility of getting the youngest two to bed and getting Dad's tea – I had to do it! I was a surrogate mum for my baby sister Wendy and used to bottle feed her through the night when I was nine years old. Mum had amazing friends from her factory jobs and went on 'work do' coach holidays to Margate. She'd take me with her to Dreamland, Margate, when I was 13 to 15 as a way to say thank you for everything I did at home. As we got older, Mum had a day job at Klingler's in North Cray, manufacturing engine gaskets. One time, she went on a drinking 'work do' coach trip and my dad followed her on his motorbike. They had a big row; whether she was seeing someone, I don't know! Dad made her get on the bike and he rode her home. She wouldn't speak to him. 'Tell your father his tea is ready!' we'd hear each night for weeks! Mum stayed at Klinger's until she was made redundant in the mid-80s. She started to get some chesty coughs and breathing difficulties due to the asbestos dust on the gaskets.

Rows are inevitable when you have been married for a while and have four kids. I used to put my fingers in my ears to block all the shouting and cursing. Mum and Dad always made up, often by snogging, with Mum on Dad's lap. We would be sent to bed early so they could enjoy the throes of passion. Mum was so short and Dad so tall and slim, they looked an unlikely couple. Mum used to say, 'We're the same height lying down!'

When my sister Wendy was still a baby, Mum and Dad had an enormous row, probably around the lack of money, as only Dad was working at that time, as a docker at Woolwich Docks.

Mum was sobbing and told me and Jackie to go and pack a bag. Wendy was in the pram and Jimmy was sitting by the push handle. Jackie and I were quite excited; it wasn't often we went on an adventure. 'Where are we going, Mum?' we chorused. 'To see your aunty Mary and uncle Tommy in Cotmandene,' she said. Cotmandene was a very long walk – OK for Wendy and Jimmy in the pram, but for me and Jackie . . . we started to cry. 'What about Dad? Who's going to look after Sooty (our cat)?' Mum started pushing the pram.

'Kath! Kath!! Get back in here, you silly cow! It's dark and cold! Don't go now. You can go in the morning!' Dad began to shout. The next thing I remember is Mum and Dad kissing in the kitchen. I was so disappointed; I thought we were going on an adventure. 'Put Jimmy and Wendy to bed,' said Mum. 'Where's me dinner?' said Dad. 'In the cat,' said Mum.

We never did go to Cotmandene. Mum and Dad continued to forgive each other, time after time.

We played our part in rows too. We used to play pick up 2s and Ludo, but the year we got Monopoly, we rowed so much that my mum threw the whole lot in the bin!

Mum's mum, Nanny Ada Meadows.

Mum's Dad, Earnest Meadows.

Mum's family, Nanny Ada in the middle, in the white dress, surrounded by her 'munchkin sized' family.

Earnest, Ada, with mum's sister, Ada, holding her dad's hand and her brother Edward (Ted) in her mum's arms.

Top left to right: Nanny Ada and Mum's sister, Ada. Centre: Mum and their infamous dog 'Nigger'.

Mum on the right, working at Klinger's.

THE YEARLY DECENT MEAL

On a regular basis, Dad would go to his mum's (Nanny Nell) for a cooked meal, especially after a row; Mum would always say, 'Go back to your mother's then.'

Jackie and I also enjoyed Nan's meals every Saturday. We'd sit with her and Grandad Albert for sausage and mash with beans and gravy, and we always had a pudding. Nanny Nell made her own pastry, her apple pie and custard was to die for! We'd joke it was our weekly decent meal!

Mum offered lumpy mashed potatoes and burnt or under-cooked meals. We'd watch her burn sausages under the grill, as if she was in a daydream.

I would make quick and easy meals for the kids most of the time.

One fateful day, Mum brought home some pig hearts, probably from some dodgy dealer. Mum wouldn't usually dream of cooking something elaborate. She had never cooked pig hearts before.

They were still raw inside and she made us eat them. 'You will bloody eat them!' she shouted. 'I've spent ages preparing and cooking. You're not getting down from the table until every piece is gone.' Jackie cried and I threw up. To this day, I cannot

FOR GOD'S SAKE, MOTHER!

look at hearts without remembering the smell and taste of these organs.

We were hungry often; we'd open up the larder and there wouldn't be much in there. But at Christmas time, we'd have a stocking full of fruit and nuts! We'd stuff the lot in our mouths at first light. I was so sick one Christmas after eating chocolate and an orange first thing in the morning!

Dad would cook every Christmas, to give Mum a day off, which was a bit of a joke, as she didn't do a lot any other day of the year! Dad's Christmas dinner had all the trimmings and gravy, which he made from the meat juices – no lumps to be found. There were crispy roast potatoes and even sprouts.

The only downside: Jackie and I had to do all the clearing up. We didn't get time off, not even for Christmas. Not like Mum, who would sit down in the chair and drink endless glasses of port or sherry or anything that Dad would pour her.

Mum loved gammon steak, scampi and tinned salmon, but now eats what the carers put in front of her. She wouldn't think about getting herself something simple like beans on toast. She's never been a healthy eater – she adds vinegar to everything, even Oxtail soup! Maybe that's the secret to long life, add vinegar to meals.

Now Mum has ready meals from Marks & Spencer. The meals rarely come with vegetables, though Jackie picks the steam packs up from M&S. It's pot luck if the carer has time to microwave them.

Cheers, mum! Christmas 2019.

Left to right: Me, our Nanny Nell and Jackie.

A LITTLE ABOUT ME

I first met Pete at the yearly Christmas party at Klinger's. Mum would take me to say thanks for all the work I did at home looking after the house and my younger siblings! I went to the party with my school friend Annette. Pete was there with his friend Barry. I hooked up with Pete and Annette went with Barry! My dad was furious when we told him I was pregnant. By legal rights, Pete should have been arrested for child abuse, but it was 1969, the era of free sex and rock 'n' roll!

The rows at home became more and more heated with my dad, who thought his eldest had let him down. I had wanted to be a vet and travel to Africa to work with elephants, tigers and lions. Not long before my 16th birthday, I miscarried, which, God forgive me, was a big relief. I wasn't ready for a baby.

Dad was more than happy to let me go and let another man look after me. He signed the marriage papers and the wedding was arranged for four months later.

I couldn't wait to marry Pete, and the days seemed to drag until finally, we tied the knot at Woolwich registry office in 1970. I followed in Mum's footsteps by marrying at a very young age. I have been married to Pete for over 50 years, sharing the same wedding date as Mum and Dad, the 28th of November. I was 16 and Pete was 21. We ended up living with his mum and dad for over eight months before a flat became available, over a shoe repair shop. At four pounds a week, it was a lot of money for us at the time. Pete was working for WH Smith's railway bookstalls. I worked in London as a cashier for Halifax Building Society, even though I had bunked off from school when I should have been sitting my Maths CSE to meet up with Pete!

Five months before my 19th birthday, we had our first daughter, Donna. Times were hard, but we managed to get a mortgage and bought a house together. When Donna was four, we presented her with a baby sister, Kerry. Despite all the happiness, I felt with my family, I felt I'd let my dad down, as I'd intended to travel the world looking after animals.

Here's Looking at You, Mum

Memories for me and Jackie include school lunchtimes; we'd go upstairs and shake the mound lying in the bed. 'MUM!!' we'd shout. Sometimes, it would take a couple of attempts to rouse her. 'Fetch my purse,' she'd say and she would give us a 2-bob bit, around 10p in today's money. We would run down the road and buy a small loaf of bread and a tin of soup. We'd heat this on the cooker covered in past spillages, before bolting our lunch down and getting back to school before the bell went for afternoon lessons. Mum would still be in bed when we left. Those were the days of 'put up, shut up'.

'Mum, you're too old for miniskirts. You're in your 40s!' we'd try to tell her. As kids, we used to be disgusted at the length of

Mum's tight miniskirts! She was a chubby-legged, short woman, but she'd even wear the skirts to work! She loved to dye her hair black or purple, and it would sometimes go green in between where the chemicals would mix up! She'd have a huge beehive. Overnight, she'd sleep with it wrapped in a loo roll to keep the shape! I think the beehive hair was to make her look taller. Now, present-day, her nails get overgrown and misshapen and her hair is often lank and greasy, but our Wendy will give her a manicure when she visits and I will trim mum's hair when I go to see her.

Mum used to wear Nivea face cream. She loved her lipstick and foundation (we'd call it 'slap') and her trademark dangly earrings. Now, she does nothing to look after her skin.

Mum always used to love browsing charity shops to buy handbags that would hold her compact and lippy. Now, Mum doesn't think about picking up a handbag. She only uses one to hold her asthma pump, when she has to go to a medical appointment.

Now

Looking at Mum, I cannot believe she is still breathing. There she sits, in her recliner chair, all 4ft 3in of her. Mum used to be 4ft 11in, but her shrinkage to a 'munchkin-sized' mother has left her with a body that now fills her chair, with no room for the crumbs that escape from her mouth. She is now as wide as she is tall. Her short legs are like tree trunks, and due to her osteoporosis, both her feet are deformed, firstly from the bunion removal operations on both feet, but also because all her toes are bent over. Even when Mum does get out of her chair, she finds walking exceptionally difficult. We book a chiropodist, who comes to Mum's every six to eight weeks. He must be in his 80s, but he does a decent job, trimming Mum's 'hoofs', as we call them.

A lack of dental hygiene left Mum with no front teeth. She used to have a couple of crowns in her top gums. When one of them fell out, Mum got the super glue and proceeded to stick the tooth back onto the screw. We did laugh when she showed us; it was stuck on back to front.

Not long ago, she had just one front tooth left dangling from her gums, which she often tried to pull out.

'Mum, you look so much better without your wobbly tooth. Did you pull it out?' I asked.

Mum replied, 'I think I must have swallowed it.'

'I hope not, Mum. It was rather large; it may be stuck somewhere.'

'It'll probably bite my bum when I go for a poo,' she said, laughing.

Mum may have her 'diamentcha', but sometimes, her sense of humour resurfaces and can make us laugh when we least expect it.

I imagine dementia as a black veil that's come down on her brain; behind the veil is a demon, totally deleting her memories.

Pastimes at Polroad

'Mum, Dad, we have got something to tell you.'

'You're pregnant again?' asked Dad.

(Donna was 13, and Kerry was nine; we didn't want more children!)

'We've put the house on the market; we are moving to Cornwall,' I told them. They were gobsmacked.

We sold for £98,000 and bought a beautiful house in Bodmin for £20,000 less! Both girls were settled in school and Pete got a job as a postman. In a spacious and spotless home, I sat crying my eyes out. I was missing Mum and Dad, my sisters and friends. I needed something in my life and told Pete this wasn't what I wanted; I needed a vocation and if he wasn't prepared to agree, I was leaving.

Polroad Cottage became my life saver. A 17th-century mill-house with five bedrooms that was being used for bed and breakfast. It had three acres and the bonus of a holiday cottage, rented out for holiday makers.

Bed-and-breakfast guests, holiday makers in the adjoining cottage and cream teas in the garden turned out to be heaven. And the icing on the cake:

Mum and Dad came too!

I can't recall discussing it with Pete, but Mum and Dad were moved down to Cornwall to live in a mobile home in our back field! I was happy as a pig in muck. I felt like I had a second chance to make my dad proud, while keeping my parents close to me.

Dad did all the odd jobs and Mum helped with serving the cream teas and helping to clear up. She was more of a hindrance than a help, as I had to clean and hoover all the places she had missed. Mum was happy; I was exhausted.

We had goats, chickens, ducks, cats and dogs. Mum and Dad joined the Labour Club in Camelford, and every week we played darts and pool. Because Mum was so short, she could only play the lower numbers on the board. If she required a double one to finish, we'd be in hysterics for hours, Mum on her rum and coke and me on lime and soda, as I always drove. It was a once-a-week 'thank you' treat for Mum and Dad. I wish I could have given more. I would come up with any excuse to go over to their caravan and spend the evening drinking Dad's homemade 'hooch' as he called it. Dad had made his own distill using an old immersion tank. Since I'd left home at 15, having Mum and Dad around made me feel like I'd come home again.

After 12 years, Polroad became a costly chore. Pete and I made the decision to sell up, buy a bungalow and ask the council for a bungalow for Mum and Dad.

Dad was having none of it. He wanted to go back to Sidcup, to his home on the council estate. I was heartbroken. Saying that, Pete was happy, he had me all to himself again. I must admit, in the years Mum and Dad were there, I was giving lots of time to my parents rather than my husband.

After living in Cornwall for 22 years, Pete and I moved up to Derbyshire. We had already missed seeing Donna's children, Joe, and Amber, grow up. When Kerry had her son, I was upset to think I would miss his early life, as I had missed seeing Joe's and Amber's. Little Lewis would be five years old when we moved; we were both excited.

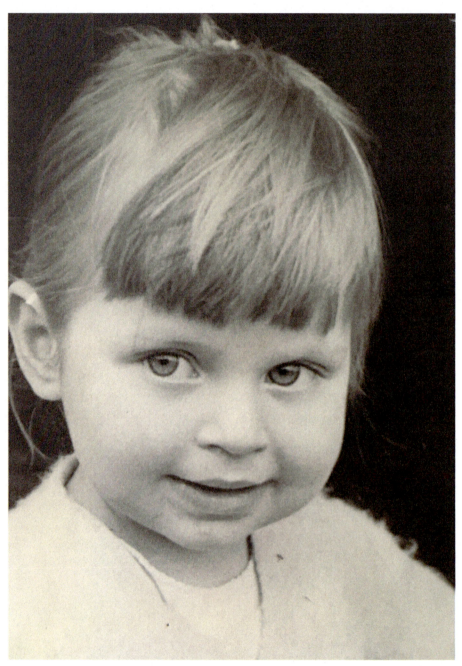

Me, aged around 3 years.

Form left to right: Wendy and Jackie, mid-1960s outside Nanny Nell's house.

From left to right: Wendy, Jimmy, Jackie and me.

28 November 1970, our wedding day.

HOME AND AWAY

Mum can't make memories now.

'Making memories' is for those without dementia. My sisters and I still want to hear Mum's laugh and see her happy, so we decided to give her a holiday before her dementia shuts her out completely. We wanted her to have an enjoyable time.

'Let's take her to the Kent coast for a four-day caravan break,' I suggested, as I planned to come down from Derby at the weekend. Arrangements were made and off we went to Romney Marsh. Jackie and Wendy in one car, and Mum and I went with my daughter Donna, in her car.

It would have been too cramped in one vehicle, what with all the luggage, alcohol, food and Mum's endless pads, medication and her wheelchair. July can be a wonderful time of year, and we soon arrived at our destination and unloaded the cars.

We got Mum settled in the caravan's lounge area whilst we unpacked. 'Where am I?' Mum asked.

'In a caravan,' I answered.

'Just for today?'

'No, Mum, Monday to Thursday!'

FOR GOD'S SAKE, MOTHER!

We gave Mum the double room closest to the loo. Mum would ask us hourly, 'When are we going home?'

'Thanks for bringing us down, Donna,' I said to my daughter.

'I'll be back to get you in four days!' Donna said.

At the end of Mum's bed was a bedspread hanging down, and Mum got her foot caught and had a fall. She had bruises on her knees and looked a bit shaken up.

The next day we went to the town center, ready to visit the charity shops, and got Mum and her wheelchair out of the car.

'I'm not getting in that. I can walk.' Mum walked a few yards before declaring, 'I will get in the wheelchair.' I have lost count of the times she has done this; she's adamant she can be independent. At least now, we could make progress and visit more shops. We were having a lovely time. Wendy and I popped into a chemist and left Jackie outside with Mum. On our return, Jackie mentioned something had happened while we were gone.

Mum had said, 'Jackie doesn't give me any money; I can't buy anything.'

Jackie had replied, 'I'm Jackie, Mum, and you have money in your purse!'

All was forgotten when we went to a tearoom and we let Mum pay!

Back at the caravan, Mum went to bed, while we girls sat outside in the sunshine, laughing, with drinks in hand. Mum appeared at the door. 'Did you have a nice sleep?' I asked. Mum stood there, and I noticed her labored breathing. Her face was worryingly white. I went in and got her to sit down. My sisters followed me in. Mum did not look good.

I rang the reception. 'Is there an onsite doctor?' I asked.

'Call 111,' they replied.

Two paramedics came within 30 minutes and suggested Mum should go to the hospital, as she had a heart rate of over 100 beats a minute (tachycardia). Poor Mum did not want to go, as she made her protests loud and clear.

'Mum is so stubborn; she won't go,' I announced to the room. I imagine I sounded bombastic, like I was telling them how to do their job. The paramedics asked me to wait outside! I joined my sisters in the sunshine.

I don't know how they did it, but Mum agreed to go to the hospital.

With Mum strapped on a bed in the ambulance and me sitting on a chair, I waved goodbye to Wendy and Jackie. 'I'll call you later!' I shouted to my sisters before the back doors were closed, and off we went to Ashford Hospital, an hour's journey away from our caravan.

It was late afternoon when we got to A&E. Mum was wired up and had various drips and needles in her arms. Mum hates needles, and as I watched the monitors and heard the beeps and blips of the machines, I began to wonder whether this was it for Mum.

Mum whimpers like a puppy at her blood tests; she absolutely hates them and her breathing gets shallower. 'Calm down, Mrs Rogers,' they always say. She has tears in her eyes when they pierce her wafer-thin skin or slap her hand when they can't find a vein. It hurts Mum. I can understand why Mum doesn't want to go to the hospital and have all the treatment.

Mum wanted to have her ears pierced as a child, but Nanny Ada had said no. Mum went to her brother, and Ted froze each ear lobe with ice cubes before inserting a needle, threaded with cotton, through her ears. Nanny Ada went mad, and our mum got a wallop. When Ted owned up to the piercings, he got a wallop too. I imagine this is where her fear of needles comes from.

'Why can't you just let me go home?' Mum said in the hospital.

I was sad but not shocked, as she'd said this before. I tried to calm her down.

'Come on, Mum. Let's play I, spy!'

'F E,' said Mum, surprisingly.

I looked around the room for clues. 'Fibrillator? Face, Female?'

Mum had her poker face on and kept replying with a short, sharp no.

Fifteen minutes later, I gave up.

Mum pointed (to the wall directly in front of us) to a sign that read, 'Fire Exit.'

I burst out laughing.

'Why are you laughing?' Mum kept asking.

'Because it was funny, Mum,' I said as my heart warmed from the moment we'd shared.

At one o'clock in the morning, I was ringing Jackie to come and pick us up. Mum's heart rate was back to normal; they were not keeping her in, but we would have to inform her doctor as soon as we got home.

We were waiting near the exit at 2 a.m. when Wendy ran in and said Jackie had parked just around the corner, but the heater in her car was playing up and she was on the phone with her husband, Terry. Jackie was advised to drive with the windows down to cool the car. Mum and I were in the back, and it was freezing. If Mum's heart did not kill her off, freezing to death would do it!

Halfway back, Jackie had to stop the car to fill up the water heater. Luckily for us, a man also stopped. He was our knight in shining armor. He was wearing a security badge, which made it OK for us. He was brilliant and saw us on our way. We arrived back at the caravan just after 3 a.m. We were all shattered. We got Mum to bed, and I must have nodded off around 4 a.m.

'What are you doing, Mum?' I woke up with a start. Mum was fully dressed, standing at the bottom of my bed, pulling off my bed covers.

'I don't know where I am,' she said. 'Where am I?'

'Go back to bed, Mum. It's not time to get up yet.' I looked at my watch: 7 a.m. I felt so sorry for Mum, standing there, with a face that said it all... She looked lost and puzzled. I wanted to cry for her. We thought we would be able to give Mum an enjoyable time and make memories for us, her daughters, but what we created was a confused and lost soul who was scared and afraid. I got up and made her a cup of tea. I would tell

Jackie and Wendy we needed to take Mum home that same day.

To add salt to the wound, the caravan site wouldn't give us a refund for our missing days.

We'd only been there a full day. It was horrible. Her last ever holiday. We can't take her away again, as she's too confused.

When Mum has gone up to Dad, we sisters have said we'll have a break ourselves to celebrate and remember our mum.

***

We didn't get many childhood holidays, but I do remember Dad playing guitar around the campfire one year at Wateringbury Farm in Kent. Dad loved Jim Reeves, so he played some oldies, but he also liked to make up songs! During the day, Jackie and I had a basket that we had to fill with hops for the farmer. Even now, I can feel that crispy little hop in my hand and the sweet earthy smell of fresh beer. Jackie was four and I was five. Our holidays were working holidays. As we got older, we'd drive down to Cornwall and pitch a tent.

In Mum's youth, she used to be so quick with the bingo dabber. You'd never know she was waiting for a number, and then she'd win the card and make you jump by shouting, 'Eee YAARR!' really loudly!

We took Mum to bingo in Derbyshire in 2018. It was the last time; we said we could never take her again. Mum kept talking and shouting, 'Eee YARR.' People kept shushing us. The announcer even told us off. 'If you're going to be too noisy, you're going to have to leave.'

People couldn't hear the numbers being called, and she'd miss a number and create a fuss. People were getting annoyed. It was serious Gala bingo! People were tutting. I wanted to say, 'She's got dementia.' I wanted to stand up for her. They should run bingo for dementia sufferers. They still want to play but by more relaxed rules!

Mum used to love watching all the TV soaps, like *Coronation Street*. She used to love horror films. I've never been able to watch them, ever since Dad played a trick on Jackie and me when we were little. We were chatting away before bed, with the door ajar to let the light in a little from the hallway. All of a sudden, the hall light turned off and a grotesque mask appeared around the door, with a torch lighting its terrifying features from the bottom. That was Dad's sense of humour!

Mum can't turn the TV on now; she'll spend hours looking out of the window. She loves watching the birds.

Mum still loves word searches, even now. If she's not sleeping, she's doing a word search. She has a stairlift, but we're thinking about moving her bed downstairs. We know we need to do it gradually. Right now, she won't hear about moving downstairs.

Mum loved her days out and in previous visits to us, we had taken her to Chatsworth House for a picnic in the park. Her walking was beginning to get more difficult, so we hired a wheelchair from St John's Ambulance. She frustratingly refused to use it, but at Chatsworth, we told her she'd get in free if she was in a wheelchair, so she sat in one! We now realise that she just wanted to stay independent. I must say that Mum was always generous with her money, but we all love something for free!

In 1987, we had a three-week holiday in America to spend some time with Mum's brother. Uncle Ted was around 60 when he met an American lady in her 30s and moved to Dallas. Uncle Ted had missed his English roast dinner, so he asked us to cook one. Well, I've never been so hot in all my life. The temperature was in the 90s, he had no air-conditioning and we had to cook on a range cooker. We cooked beef, cabbage, roast potato and Yorkshire puddings! Mum helped but we all felt ill from the heat! We decided to surprise Mum with a trip to see Elvis. Uncle Ted took us to Phoenix, where we hopped on a Greyhound bus.

The trip took over 24 hours, but we went to Graceland to see Elvis's grave. It was the 10th anniversary of his death, but there were rumors that he was still alive. She loved that trip. It was the last time Mum saw Ted, as he died at the age of 65. Mum is the sole survivor of her siblings.

Polroad Cottages, Cornwall.

SHAME ON US

We went into panic mode when Mum was first diagnosed with dementia. I look back at our behaviour now and feel ashamed of how we reacted. We took control of Mum's finances and instantly tried to put her in a home. Mum understandably fought against her three daughters taking away her independence and autonomy.

I know that Mum having carers is the right thing for her now, but in hindsight, we rushed into it to ease our guilt at not being there 24/7 to care for her. We forced Mum to have carers when she didn't need them, at that time. We did jump the gun. Knowing Mum's determination, she would have coped! We just saw the diagnosis. Wendy and I wanted Mum in a home, and Jackie fought against that. I'm ashamed of the stress we caused each other and Mum by fighting over this.

When Mum had cancer, we didn't think she had long left. I didn't think about life; I thought about death. When Mum went in to have her mastectomy, she was suffering a little from memory loss. The consultant warned us her dementia could be worse after being under the general anaesthetic. It did. It was because of the lack of oxygen to the brain. Mum didn't want her breast removed, but her doctor warned that the tumour would burst inside her. 'Look what they've done to me; they've taken my breast away,' she said after the operation. If she was younger, they would have done reconstructive surgery, but instead, they gave her a pad to put in her bra. Mum doesn't wear a bra; she wears a vest. During the day, the pad would ride up and end up under her chin! 'Take that off,' I'd say, but she would say, 'It's my breast!'

Mum stayed with us for seven months, due to COVID-19 hitting after her operation and I did not want her to be at home alone. We had a lovely Christmas in 2019; Mum laughed a lot, drank a lot and wet the chair twice! On New Year's Eve, we sat out on the patio, burning logs and toasting the New Year with a drink in hand.

I took care of Mum's personal needs, from washing her to dressing her. 'Look what they have done to me,' she'd say endlessly.

'But you're still alive, Mum,' I'd repeat often.

***

One day, while she was with us, Mum decided to go for a walk in the park to get out of the chair for a bit – she had begun to put weight on.

'Is Mum still in the park?' I'd asked Pete, 20 minutes later. 'I know she's slow, but...' Pete went out into the park and after a few minutes he was back. 'I can't see her,' he said. My heart sank. 'Where is she? She should have been back by now. Go look round the back, and I'll go search for her out the front.' All sorts of things were going through my mind: she may have been abducted! Though who would want to abduct an 84-year-old who is fit for nothing, I don't know. She may have been lost or lying injured somewhere... She may have been DEAD!!

'She's here!' I heard Pete shouting. There was Mother with a grin on her face. 'Where the fuck have you been? We've been worried sick.'

'For a walk,' she said.

'But you've been gone for over an hour. You've got dementia! Anything could have happened!' I shouted.

'Well, I'm all right aren't I? Don't know what all the fuss is about!'

After the string of obscenities that came out of my mouth, I should have been locked up for verbal abuse.

I listened to Jackie's phone ringing. 'Come on, answer,' I said to myself.

'Oh, hi, Jan,' Jackie said.

'Hello, Jack. I'm sorry, but I can't cope with her anymore' – the words of defeat I thought I'd never say.

'OK, what's happened?'

Sobbing, I managed, 'This is the final straw...' I told her about Mum going missing for an hour.

'You'll have to bring her home,' Jackie said, lowering her tone on the phone. Shame gnawed at my insides. *I couldn't cope with her.* My inner critic was screaming, *I'm her eldest; it's my responsibility! For God's sake, Mother! I feel so bad.*

I have hated myself for snapping at her. She can't help it; it's the demon within her. I hate remembering how I couldn't cope and wanted her to go home. The more I've written about Mum, the more I've realised how selfish I've been towards her. There have been a lot of times when I've said that Mum's 'playing us up' as if she's a naughty toddler. Recently, Lionel did all her washing and hung it up wet, and Mum began to fold it up! 'For God's sake, Mother!' we'd chastise her, as if she knows what she's doing. But she doesn't know.

How I wish we could be as happy as we were when this picture was taken. From left to right: Me, Wendy and Jackie.

SID

Although Mum said, 'No more dogs', in the year 2000, Dad went to view some rescues at Biggin Hill. A two-year-old white and tan dog came over and dropped a ball at Dad's feet. That was it; Dad was in love. 'I'll have that one,' he said.

Dad showed his love through his dogs, and Sid was Dad's constant companion. Every time Dad had a cup, he'd say, 'It's Sidcup!' as in, 'Sid's cup.' Sid was named after where they lived. He would pour some tea into Sid's bowl. Sid was what we called a Heinz 57 dog – lots of varieties!

Dad would wear Sid out using a ball thrower; Sid would always find the ball (even in the river!) and take it back to Dad, only for it to be thrown again and again. Dad would open the door and say, 'Cats!' even if there were none in the garden; Dad would laugh at how manic Sid was in his mission to find that cat. Dad had emphysema in his later years so resorted to using a mobility scooter. He would take Sid down to Five Arches, a beautiful woodland park with its own river. As time went on, Dad's health declined and he struggled to get around; eventually, he had to go on oxygen.

Dad, ever the character, would smoke rollies, saying, 'Lovely fag!' even when he was on oxygen! Sid would sit beside him, unaware of the explosive risk of the oxygen and a lit cigarette!

Things became serious in 2007. Dad didn't sleep upstairs; he always slept in a chair downstairs with Sid. My mum came down one morning and Dad was dead, on the floor, by the radiator. *Maybe he'd been cold in the night*, I've pondered in the years since. Sid was curled up by my dad on the floor. After the funeral, Mum never mentioned my dad; she only mentioned Sid. Sid was a big part of Dad, and I can understand why Mum didn't want to let Sid go too, Sid was a reminder of Dad.

Even when Dad was alive, Sid began to put on weight. As well as Sid's regular cuppas, he'd have a pre-dunked biscuit fed to him at least once a day. After Dad died, Mum didn't take Sid for walks.

In 2018, we had to tell Mum that Sid was ready to go and be with Dad.

'He's OK. He's eating. He'll still chase the cats out of the garden!' Mum protested.

'But he's 19 now. He's in pain, Mum,' I said. Sid was covered in lumps and bumps, with a particularly bad lump over his eye. The vet had said he might not survive an operation to remove it. His sight was going. He was slowing down; he'd still chase the cats but could hardly see them!

'Mum, you can't keep the dog alive any longer. How about you spend two more weeks with Sid, then we'll have to let him go?'

When the fateful day came two weeks later, it was down to me to be with Sid. Sid was pacing up and down and couldn't breathe. My sister Jackie took Mum out for coffee.

The vet came into the garden with his injection. 'Don't worry, Sid. You'll soon be with Dad. Good boy, Sid.' I had a lump in my throat from trying to hold in all my emotions. 'Go, Sid. Go with Dad.'

I looked up and saw the cross my brother had made when Dad died – *divine intervention* – I saw it as a sign that Dad was waiting for Sid! Tears began rolling down my cheeks. I sobbed loudly as Sid's eyes finally closed for the last time.

'You're cruel. Why did you have to put the dog down?' Mum said when she returned.

Mum keeps Sid's ashes in her bedroom and when Mum has gone, she wants to have her and Sid's ashes scattered on Dad's grave. I often joke it may not be in my lifetime, as Mum is stubborn enough to live until her late 90s or early 100s, just like her two old aunts.

Are there any vets who will put down a very old, stubborn... ONLY JOKING!!!!

Occasionally, I look after a friend's dog called Ziggy. Mum hardly remembers my name but often asks, 'How's that little dog?' She remembers seeing him when she visited. It's like Mum has a tiny pile of sentences that she can pick up and use. She doesn't make new sayings anymore.

Two months after this picture was taken, Sid went to be with dad.

I'M ALRIGHT; IT'S THE OTHERS

Every time I ring Mum, I say, 'Hi, it's me, Jan,' as she doesn't recognise my voice. I ask, 'How are you?' and she'll always reply, 'I'm all right; it's the others.' That's one of her sayings! She's so deaf now, we have resorted to shouting down the phone. She refuses to wear hearing aids.

Mum's forgetfulness can be upsetting and annoying. Mum still knows we are her daughters, but I become Jackie or Wendy, and they become Janis. I have stopped saying, 'I'm Jan, Mum, not Jackie or Wendy.' What's the point in correcting her? She will forget again. The thing that puzzles me the most is she always remembers our husbands' names: Pete, my husband; Terry, Jackie's; and Phil, who is married to Wendy. She has always called Pete her chauffeur, Terry her maintenance man and Phil her chef. I can't begin to explain this!

I am learning not to keep nagging her about her forgetfulness, as she gets upset, and I get angry. I tend to agree with her to save my energy and to stop her from looking puzzled. But it can be upsetting when the photographs of many grandchildren get overlooked, as she can no longer remember who they are.

Mum should be in a medical journal. *How can one person have so many health conditions and still be alive?* I wonder.

I remember Mum going to hospital with **jaundice** when we were children. Dad couldn't look after four kids, so we were all sent to his mum's. Mum also had **depression**, probably caused by us kids. I remember her mum, Nanny Ada, spending a lot of time at our house and making sure Mum was eating and drinking. A **hysterectomy** followed in later years, which led to **bladder problems**.

Mum became **'chesty'** just before leaving Klinger's in the '80s. She's had many stays in hospital for '**lack of breath**'. Mum has her own nebuliser, which she's forgotten how to use. The asthma pumps help with her breathing. Mum also has **COPD**, which has caused **fluid on her lungs and an enlarged heart.** It's a wonder she is still alive. Not like poor Dad, who died of heart failure when he was only 74. Mum's illnesses are clinging on to her for better or for worse.

Osteoporosis is the cause of all Mum's pain and discomfort. Mum has considerable shrinkage of the spine – hence why we call her 'Mummy Munchkin'. Mum's left **wrist was broken** after she fell while being mugged in a telephone box in Portugal.

The right wrist break came about when Mum tripped over a bag of apples that Dad had left on the kitchen floor. We don't know how she didn't see them; she is nearer to the ground than any of us! Most of Mum's pain is in her feet, another reason why she doesn't like to walk. She's **had both knees replaced**!

Mum is now **obese**, considering her height of 4ft 3in, a killer in its own right. Most of Mum's problems are now due to being so overweight; it is aggravating all of her health conditions. It is a vicious cycle. Mum won't get out of the chair because it hurts her back, she doesn't want to walk because it hurts her feet and if she doesn't get out of the chair, she wets herself. And so it goes on, round and round in circles. I remember when Mum was a size 10; now, we have to buy trousers in a size 16.

You Have a Choice, Mum: Carers or a Home?

We decided to find out about having carers after my sisters and I found her cold and almost dead on the sofa that fateful day I mentioned at the beginning of this book. The fact she perked up and asked for porridge while the three of us and two paramedics tried to convince her she needed to go to hospital was beside the point.

Perhaps she did have the onset, at that time, but it was several years later when we got the diagnosis, after Mum had a brain scan. I sat with Mum on a Zoom call, and it was revealed then that she'd had bleeding on the brain; the words **vascular dementia** rang in my ears. Little did we know, as sisters, that this diagnosis was now our 'diagnosis': a diagnosis of caring for Mum and suffering alongside her.

Mum's sister, Ada, died at 83 after having breast and womb cancer; she also had dementia. Ada had been told by the doctor she needed to drink more water. She thought that she had to drink water all the time. She'd pick up any glass of water from the care home she was in and drink the water. She'd even pick up vases, take the flowers out and drink the water. She drank so much that she washed the minerals from her body. Mum's now 87 and can't remember her siblings.

The Carers

'I can take care of myself!' Mum said when my sisters and I suggested carers.

When they first came along, speaking in foreign accents with masks on, Mum couldn't understand what they were saying.

The first carers Mum started off with seemed fine, even though Mum hated the idea. We only wanted morning and lunchtime, and instructions were given about Mum's medication, what she liked to eat and drink and Mum's need to have her hair washed at least once a week. Sadly, this didn't happen.

This company was not giving Mum her pills, not understanding our instructions for Mum's asthma medication and not giving her adequate food. In the beginning, it was written in her care plan that a carer would give Mum 45 minutes in the morning for washing, dressing and giving her breakfast; 15 minutes for lunch time, for a sandwich or soup and a cup of tea; and, when Mum had evening carers, 30 minutes to do her a ready meal. The carers put false times in the logbook, and Mum often had a sandwich at lunchtime and then a sandwich again at teatime. They were in and out. Sometimes, Mum didn't even have a hot drink.

Social Services listened to my list of complaints and it was not long before the second care company got in touch.

'Brilliant news!' I told Jackie and Wendy. 'Mum will be getting a main carer.' Someone Mum could get used to.

The carer washed Mum's hair and made her laugh, she came three times a day and built rapport with Mum.

Lionel was hoovering Mum's bedroom and noticed the two-pound jar was low on coins. We wondered if Mum had been taking it, and if she had, where was it? We looked in her safe, under the bed and in her bedroom drawers, but there was no money to be found. We figured out that the money had been stolen. That was the moment we decided to get in cameras.

Using the cameras, we saw a carer going into Mum's little silver box. Jackie moved all temptation out of reach. It seemed strange the main carer stopped her visits to Mum, she didn't return, and the care company said they had no one in the area to come out to her. We were fuming! So, it went out for tender again through Social Services.

We were left for six weeks with different carers, so I called the council to have a strong word. The day after I complained, relief washed over me when Social Services rang. They had good news: a new care company would be in the very next day. We are now happy with Mum's new care provider. There are often two carers dealing with Mum's needs, and Jackie gets phone calls from the carers if they are going to be late or if Mum refuses to get up. They do make sure she takes the right number of pills, which is reassuring for us, as Mum has taken two lots in one go before now.

I was there just after Christmas, when the third lot of carers arrived. I was lying in my bedroom, and Mum began shouting, 'You can't make me get out of bed!'

I was angry, so I went into her room and pulled her covers off. 'You've got to get up, Mum. These people cannot wait around all day,' I said. She got up and slammed the bathroom door behind her and locked it.

'Don't worry! We're used to people not wanting help!' the carers said to me before leaving. I stood at the door, watching them get in their car.

'Yoo hoo, yoooo hoo! Help! I can't get my vest on!' Mum shouted to me from the top of the stairs.

I ran up the stairs. 'That's tough, Mum. The carers have already gone! You'll have to do it yourself!' I shouted angrily. Mum slammed the door on me this time.

I left her room and went down the stairs. By the time I got back to the living room, I'd broken down and was crying my eyes out. My frustration at Mum was too much for me to bear; I had been so cruel.

'Isn't it a lovely day?' Mum said as she came into the lounge as if nothing had happened; our conflict was forgotten.

The ironic thing is, although Mum didn't remember it, I'll regret my behavior forever. I now know that I must stand back and be like a carer, be neutral. As the carers said, they are used to dealing with the elderly. There was no need for me to get angry.

FOR GOD'S SAKE, MOTHER!

Vascular dementia is caused by reduced blood flow to the brain, which damages and eventually kills brain cells. This can happen as a result of narrowing and blockage of the small blood vessels inside the brain or a single stroke, where the blood supply to part of the brain is suddenly cut off. (nhs.co.uk)

From left to right: Jackie, Wendy and me with Mum in the centre.

BUT I'M STILL ALIVE!

Thinking back to my childhood, I remember the frost used to be on the insides of the windows; we had no double glazing, just glass in old metal frames. We used to play outside with socks on our hands because we didn't have gloves. Inside was the lingering smell of Dad's rollies. Jackie and I would get tobacco on our fingers from going through Dad's pockets for change to buy peanut brittle!

Dad used to joke that our front room carpet was more shag pile than Worcester; we remember it as a stagnant pile with the aroma of dog! Sid particularly hated the hoover, but he didn't have to worry too much, as Mum didn't often use it!

'Move back!' Mum would shout when she poured the boiling water in the bath for Jackie and me. We didn't have a water heater or any central heating, so she'd need to boil the water on the stove.

Mum would run the bath for Dad, and Jackie and I would have his water; then she'd put in Jimmy and Wendy, after we had got out. The good old days of bathing in each other's filth! I had our bath taken out and a shower put in, as I can't stand the thought of a bath after my childhood!

After leaving home and marrying at 16, I used to visit Mum and Dad's and I'd see how disgusting it really was. I'm completely the opposite of mum and a bit of a 'neat freak'; if my husband gets out of the chair, I'm plumping the cushion. I think that my OCD has come from living in a pigsty. Mum would never see it; I used to clean the toilet before my kids would use it and I'd take my own disinfectant with me wherever I went. Mum has had no sense of smell for as long as I can remember. Her brown, drab furniture was never cleaned, and Mum wouldn't dream of dusting. If one of us wet the bed, Mum would put the sheets through the mangle and hang them to dry. She wouldn't think about washing them.

Before Mum's dementia set in, we would remind her of things from our childhood and she'd say, 'But I'm still alive!' I suppose if she ate a tonne of dirt, she probably would still survive because she has an immunity to dirt! Mum caught COVID, and we thought, *Right, this is it*. Mum was as right as rain!

Mum's aunt Daisy and aunt Vi lived until their early hundreds!! I don't know if I'd survive the stress of another 23 years of Mum.

Thank Goodness for Cousins

Mum has a pale grey sofa now and down the side of her chair is very messy; there are stains on the arms. If she spills tea, she won't think to get a cloth! Wendy and I recently had a conversation about finding someone who would clean Mum's toilets and hoover and polish, as Mum's physical ability to clean has absolutely diminished now. She couldn't do it any longer (not that she ever tried). Donna, my daughter, initially started doing the housework, but with increasing work pressures and the fact she could only do it fortnightly, we thought it was time to find someone who could come twice a week.

I decided to give my cousin Lionel a ring. This wasn't going to be that easy, as we'd had a falling out a while ago.

'Hello, Lionel! It's me, Janis.'

'Oh, hello,' he said. 'You're going to speak to me now, are you?'

I wasn't sure how this falling out had gone on for so long. I loved my cousins; as kids, we would play over in Five Arches for hours.

I stumbled over a feeble apology, hoping the past could be forgiven. 'I was just wondering if Pat (Lionel's partner) would like a cleaning job? We're looking for a cleaner for Mum.'

Luckily for us, Pat and Lionel were no longer working. They now come on Monday and Thursday mornings. Lionel does all the hoovering, while Pat does the rest. The house always smells nice. It's a pleasure to go to Mum's knowing the house is clean and hygienic. It's not just the housekeeping that they do; they also keep an eye on Mum. They've even put plastic covers on the arms of the chairs for Mum's spillages!

Lionel looked after his own mum and dealt with her personal care, while Pat's mum has dementia too. They were sent from God to help us with Mum. We are so grateful.

Mum loved to pose.

PRESENT DAY

Mum's 87. I check in on her several times a day, via the camera. She is asleep in her chair late at night, still in the clothes she's worn all day. Jackie, Wendy and I have now decided to get Mum a single recliner bed and have it downstairs.

One Saturday night, at 7 p.m., I looked at the camera app on my mobile. Mum was opening her front room curtains after they had been closed. *How strange.* I waited for Mum to get back in her chair and as I watched her, fully clothed, reclining her chair and turning out her lamp, I realised she was settling down for the night. I decided to ring her. Keeping the camera app on, I watched her reaching over and picking up the phone.

'Hello, Mum. You OK?'

'Yeah, I'm all right; it's the others.'

'What are you up to, Mum? Are you watching telly?'

Knowing full well she wasn't, she replied, 'I'm reading a book.'

'Oh! What's it about, Mum?'

'I don't know,' she replied, and then she asked, 'What's the time? Is it morning or night?'

'Look out the window, Mum, and tell me if it's dark or light.'

Mum looked out the window. 'It's dark. It must be night-time.'

'And what is your clock showing, Mum?'

I watched Mum's head turn to look at the digital clock, which tells not only the time but also the date, day and whether it's a.m. or p.m.

'It's 10 past seven. It must be night-time.'

I asked her if she was going to bed and reminded her not to sleep in the chair, as she would wake up with a backache.

'I'll go up to bed when I have read another chapter of my book,' she said.

'OK, Mum. I'll ring you tomorrow. Nighty night.'

'Thanks for ringing, love,' she said. I watched her as she pulled her fleece blanket up to her chin and turned the light off.

Another time, I noticed on the camera feed that she was having an animated conversation on the phone. As she was so happy, I called after I saw her put the phone down and asked, 'Who were you talking to, Mum?'

'I don't know!' she replied.

We got Mum a clock that shows the day of the week because after her mastectomy, she no longer knew the days of the week. She still asks us if it's day or night. I find myself saying, 'Look out of the window,' but Mum just needs us to tell her the answer, not to test her.

So much has changed since Mum's diagnosis of vascular dementia. She is not the fun-loving 'Mummy Munchkin' she was. Mostly, Mum seems to be on another planet. It's become rarer to see her funny side. Her frustration, anger and temper (part of the illness) bring out our own frustration, anger and sadness (normal reactions). It's harder, yet more important than ever, to put into place the lessons we've learnt in the past few years.

Just last month, I watched Mum on the camera brushing her hair and putting on her face cream. She spent a long time folding her nightdress, getting all the seams together just so. My heart sank as she sat down and began the process of brushing her hair and putting on her cream again. She'd forgotten what she'd just done.

Then sometimes, she'll surprise us by making herself a cup of tea!

Mum sleeps for longer and longer these days; her sense of time, dates, days and nights has disappeared. All we can do is hold her in the darkness of her 'diamentcha' and wish that demon goes on its way.

***

When I visited Mum at Christmas in 2020, her carers arrived in the afternoon with a tray of cakes.

'Hey Kat-leen,' the carers greeted Mum.

I cringed. Mum hates people using her full name.

'Which cake would you like, Kat-leen?' the black carer offered.

'Eenie meenie miney mo...' Mum said, looking at the tray.

I held my breath, thinking back to the innocent rhyme from our childhood that had become extremely racist now.

FOR GOD'S SAKE, MOTHER!

Mum was hovering her finger over a choice of two cakes, '...catch a nigger by his toe.' Mum made her choice.

I was mortified. Most of Mum's carers were black and although she was against having carers in the beginning, their colour made no difference to her. She wasn't racist, but she'd just said 'nigger' to a black person; God knows how that poor carer felt. I wanted the ground to swallow me up.

'Mum, you can't say that,' I said once the carers had gone.

'Say what?'

'"Catch a nigger"!'

'I never said that,' Mum said.

'You did, Mum!'

Mum then burst out laughing.

I've accepted that her sense of humour is part of Mum, and her language is tied to the 1930s and '40s, before political correctness.

***

Mum has so much support around her in terms of our cousins and carers and elder grandchildren, my sisters and I have noticed that we've taken on different, complementary roles to help Mum. We fended for ourselves when we were younger and we are caring for Mum now.

Jackie, who lives closest to Mum, is Mum's main carer, so she has many practical tasks to deal with, like reading the gas and electric meters, plus taking Mum to all her appointments. Wendy is a pharmacist at Chelmsford Hospital, so we call her to check on side effects of medications. I take care of Mum's phone, internet and Rayburn cooker, and because I'm not there all the time, I can spend quality time with her. Sadly, because Jackie is closest, her quality time with Mum seems to have been replaced by practical tasks. Instead of their weekly trip to the garden centre, it's the regular doctor's visits instead.

We sisters have power of attorney. Jackie feels she has to do it all. I feel she doesn't need to, as I'm only a few hours away. Jackie deals directly with Mum's day-to-day finances in a way I don't always agree with. When we go to do Mum's garden, she only has rubbish-quality rubbish bags, whereas I feel that Mum would be better off with a £40-a-year green bin for garden rubbish, but Jackie disagrees, so we clash over things like that.

My heart goes out to only-children who have to deal with a parent with dementia. Our skill sets have married up well to cope with Mum; there's three of us immediate family, plus more cleaning and supporting, yet this is still the biggest challenge we've had to face. There are support groups available, but a lot of the groups have been closed since the first lockdowns began.

Alzheimer's versus Vascular Dementia

Has your loved one been diagnosed with vascular dementia?
Please don't assume, as we did, that life is instantly over. From the day of diagnosis, we made the mistake of wanting to place Mum in a home. We took charge of her finances and took her rights away. It has been nearly four years since dementia came into our lives. For the first two, we just took over her life

and didn't take into account Mum's feelings. *Did we really bully her into having carers and take over her finances? I cry just thinking about her own personal loss of not being able to do what she used to. I would hate for my own daughters to do that to me. Shame on us, and shame on the cruel illness that has come into all our lives.*

My thoughts and feelings change on a regular basis, feelings of despair and hopelessness for Mum. Does she have any of these feelings of doom and gloom? How does she feel? What has this illness done to her? Why can't she remember?

How we got the diagnosis

Jackie was with Mum when she had a brain scan in Kent in 2018. Mum came up to me afterwards, and we had a follow-up call on Zoom with the clinician. Mum was compos mentis, but she wasn't taking the diagnosis in. 'What does it mean?' she asked me. 'It means that your memory is going to get worse, Mum,' I said. 'I'll be all right. I can remember a lot of things,' she said, defiantly. 'I've got diamentcha,' she says now, as if it was a bout of diarrhoea!

Vascular dementia is a term applied to a group of symptoms that impact the memory. Mum's illness has been caused by several mini strokes, caused by blood flow blockages in her brain, which, according to her report, have resulted in a build-up of plaque in her arteries. I thought plaque was a build-up of various food matter found on teeth, and as Mum is practically toothless, hers must have escaped to her brain.

Alzheimer's disease is a specific progressive illness that causes a slow impairment in memory and cognitive function. Unlike vascular dementia, the cause is unknown, and there is no cure available. What's even more upsetting is the fact more younger people are now being diagnosed with Alzheimer's. Vascular dementia and Alzheimer's can have the same symptoms, which include a decline in the ability to think, a decline in memory and communication impairment.

But unlike vascular dementia, other symptoms of Alzheimer's can include apathy, depression, disorientation, confusion and difficulty in speaking or swallowing. Some types of dementia will share some Alzheimer's symptoms, but not all, and diagnosis can be made difficult due to the similarities and differences. We only found out about Mum's condition due to the results of her brain scan.

Mum is not on any specific dementia medication; she rattles enough as it is. At Mum's time of life, I question the point of prolonging this illness that she doesn't even remember she has.

Mum with great-granddaughter Amber (front) and her great-great-granddaughters, Charlotte and Skye.

Mum's eldest great-grandchildren, Joe and Amber.

Jimmy's children. Granddaughter Jodie (left), their mother Angie (centre) and grandson Jamie (right).

Ben and Joanne, Mum's grandchildren.

Mum's great-grandchildren, Evie and Riley.

Great-grandson, Lewis.

Granddaughters Donna (front) and Kerry (rear), and great-great-granddaughters Charlotte (front) and Honey.

Mum's daughters, granddaughters, great-grandson, great-granddaughters and son-in-law, Pete.

THE POEM

Any time we get angry with Mum, we read a poem by Owen Darnell. Darnell is an American poet, whose wife had dementia. I found his poem on Facebook and it helps us remember that she doesn't understand much of what's going on. She needs our patience and understanding – not out anger and frustration.

In closing, I'd like to thank you for reading this book I've written from the heart. I was very close to my mum. I am close to her now, but because she has lost so much of her memory, our relationship is different. I feel like I've lost the person sitting right in front of me. Mum used to have such a big sense of fun; we're lucky to see glimpses of that now. We cherish the moments when our mum seems to come back to us momentarily.

Life is funny, it's complicated, it's sad, it's joyous and it's frustrating. Nobody knows how long we're going to be here, so we make the most of it! Life is all about making memories.

As Mum can't make memories, I store them on these pages.

FOR GOD'S SAKE, MOTHER!

Alzheimer's Request
by Owen Darnell

Do not ask me to remember,
don't try to make me understand,
let me rest and know you're with me,
kiss my cheek and hold my hand.

I'm confused beyond concept,
I'm sad, sick and lost,
all I know is that I need you,
to be with me at all cost.

Do not lose your patience with me,
do not scold, curse or cry.
I can't help the way I'm acting,
I can't be different, though I try.

Just remember that I need you
that the best of me is gone,
please don't fail to stand beside me,
love me till my life has gone.

We love you so much, Mum. We wish we could turn back time to happier days.

Story Terrace

Printed in Great Britain
by Amazon